Invisible Horizon:
A Religious Pamphlet

Sibyl Kempson

12 Shouts to the Ten Forgotten Heavens was a short-term-long-term commitment to the operations of the cosmos. An effort to resurrect the efforts of the advanced ancient civilizations who knew how to take part in what was up with Mother Universe, most of whom have been crushed by the forces of denial-of-cyclical-cycles, pursuit-of-immortality, fear-of-death, domination-over-what-one-cannot-understand, Capitalism, Colonialism, White Supremacy, or what-have-you. Basically the forces of linear logic. Spirits, and ancestors, and celestial beings and bodies, and the voices of plant, stone, and animal people came to us in different ways and asked us to reunite with and honor them. We said, "But we don't know how." And they said, "Well, figure it out!!" And so whatever time of day or night, we showed up at the Museum, and we did what we could to try, to help the process, we fell in love, we were given visions, and we took part. For three years, we took responsibility for the movement of the Earth in relation to the Sun, the cycles of the Moon, the transits of all the planets and seasons, and the well-being of all things living and growing. We met each time the Earth is closest to, farthest from, and with our Equator perfectly balanced in relation to the Sun, which is four times for each revolution around the Sun, and there were three revolutions around the Sun after we started. We took up the ropes. We retold stories that were fed to us when we were young. We went crazy. We did what we could. We proliferated, we layered. We imitated. We recreated. We tried to imagine, to envision, to intuit. It was really confusing and complicated and not clear or organized or easy. We sang and danced and spoke to presences that we couldn't see that lived in—or in the immediate environment of—the Museum. We watched the shadows of the ghosts caught on security cameras, and presented choreographed communications to them. We tried to put better images into the world from there, using that museum as our headquarters. For most of it, there was no supervision. We were like an orphanage—an orphanage that makes stuff. We fell in love in a big way. In a way that is not just personal, and not just cultural or artistic. We fell in love in a way that is mythic. We got involved in a love affair with the cosmos. It has been torrid and tumultuous. Searching our hearts for so long. Love is a battlefield. What we learned is. If it isn't for us, if we don't participate, the seasons will not have turned. We will still not be able to see what is being revealed. So... you know, man up. Own up. Heads up.

My name is _____. My role in this project has been _____.

Kira Alker – Performer, Lady Sasquatch, Sister-Goddess of Autumn & Winter Choreography

Sophia Al-Maria – Special Guest, Wisdom, Saint

Rolls André – Performer, Mother

Nivalda Assunção – Assistance in 3D Printing

Eryk Aughenbaugh – Performer, Savior, Saint

Maria Baranova – Video Documentation & Portraiture

Jared Bark – Set Design, Maker of Forests

Dee Dorcas Beasnael – Performer, High Priestess, Wielder of Clangers, Props Maker

Leonie Bell – Stage Management, Props Assistance, Montager of Ancient Sub-Aquatic Video Temples

James Benson – Video

Jeff Bergstrom – Engineer of the Audio/Visual, Neptune/Poseidon, Bringer of Redemption

Gail Blobner – Knitter of Winter Leaves

Tei Blow – Performer, Atlantean, High Priest of Sound Design

Suzanne Bocanegra – Goddess of Costume Design & Construction

Donna Brickwood – Performer, Guidance for Journeying, Mentress

Judy Breese – Knitter of Winter Leaves

Maria Camia – Animator of the Violet Flame

Tymberly Canale – Performer, Deer Woman, Ghost Choreography

Ashley Chen – Designer of Potato Doll Beings, Tree Kiosk & Phallus Construction Assistance

Max Chester – Performer, Overseer, Community Fire Keeper

WooJae Chung – Performer, Hero, Intriguing Stranger, Steward of the Trees

Hye Young Chyun – Performer, Priestess, Extra-Terrestrial Crafts Teacher, Props Mastery

Paula Court – Photographer, Visual Accompaniment

Rainer Cuiffo – Performer, Future Savior

Nora Daly – Production Assistance, Goodwill Ambassador

Amanda Davis – Coordinator of Exhibitions, Protector of Collective Dreams, Shepherdess for Neptune/Poseidon

Helga Davis – Performer, Goddess

Lenore Doxsee – Lighting Design, Kindred Spirit, Remembered

Eric Dyer – Maestro of Nautical Macramé

Darlene Farris Labar – Performer, Atlantean, Teacher, Maker of Sacred Seeds & Flowers

Johnny Gasper – Sound Assistance, Fone Fixer, Wielder of Rolling Speakers, Constant Prince

Lucas Gonzalez – Sound & Video Master Technician, Ship Captain

Anne Gridley – Performer, First Woman, Equal of Adam

Lola Harney – Doula of Performance, Keeper of Secret Knowledge & Ways, Shepherdess for Neptune/Poseidon

Camille Harris – Performer, Goddess

Greta Hartenstein – Assistant Curatrix, Performer, Advocate

Brad Hernandez – Production Assistance, Goodwill Ambassador

Lisa Holm – Performer, Mastery of Knitted Winter Leaves

Eleanor Hutchins – Performer, Fish Squid Woman

Oceana James – Performer, High Priestess, Sky Woman, Saint

Robert M. Johanson – Performer, First Man, Heir, Teacher, King

Omie Johnson – Performer, Atlantean, Astrological Dramaturgy

Sibyl Kempson – Performer, Writer, Director

Lois Lane – Set Design, Conjuror of Images

Theodora Lang – Costume Assistance, Beloved

Matt Leabo – Performer, Robots Creation

Danielle Levy – Production Assistance, Doula of Performance

Molly Lieberman – Costume Assistance, Beloved

Mo Lioce – Management of the Stage, Priestess, Bringer of Ceremonial Chitons

Ornela Lukac – Costumes Assistance, Conjuror of Priestly Robes

Elke Luyten – Performer, Hunter, Sister-Goddess of Autumn & Winter Choreography

Diana Mangaser – Designer & Maker of Bells

Sarah Matusek – Performer, Dramaturgy, Priestess, Musical Composition

Sean McElroy – Performer, Atlantean, Steward of Flowers, Rememberer of Stolen Children

Stephen McGroarty – Performer, Production Assistance, Crypto-Linguistic Researcher, Advocate, Priest

Jodi Melnick – Performer, Goddess of Spring & Summer, Choreography

Tavish Miller – Performer, Wild Man

Kat Moritz – Production Assistance, Goodwill Ambassador

Sahra Motalebi – Performer, Dramaturgy, Sound Design, Ordained

Saint, New Archetype

Oscar Noriega – Performer, Bass Clarinet, Conjuror

Brandon Alex Oakes – Performer, Contributor of Vision

Milica Paranosic – Performer, Musical Composer, Magdalene

Rachel Perks – Performer, Production Assistance, Apprentice Knitter of Winter Leaves

Max Pollak – Performer, Corporal Percussion

Alexis Powell – Musical Composition, Priestess for the Potato Doll Beings

Quartet Metadata (Lynn Bechtold, Mioi Takeda, Carrie Frey, Jennifer DeVore) – Violins, Viola, Cello

Livia Reiner – Intern, Production Assistance, Mind Journeyer

Thomas Riccio – Dramaturgy of Ritual

Victoria Roberts-Wierzbowski – Performer, Priestess of the Adonia

Kourtney Rutherford – Performer, Deer Woman

Jay Sanders – Curator, Seeker, Reeve of Original Vision

Sarah Scholl – Assistance in Stage Management & Production

Tanya Selvaratnam – Performer, Mother of all Humans

Allie Tepper – Doula of Performance, Sweetest Breeze, Shepherdess for Neptune/Poseidon

Wayne Tucker – Performer, Trumpeter

Fay Steddum – Production Assistance, Forager of Plants, Adorner of Rolling Speakers

Ruby Stenhouse – Performer, Deer Fawn

Shelly Watson – Performer, Goddess

Jessica Weinstein – Performer, Deer Woman

Jay Wegman – Performer, High Priest

Sarah Willis – Performer, Acolyte, Chosen One

Amanda Villalobos – Performer, Design & Construction of Stained Glass Windows, Tree Kiosks, Mighty Phallus, Potato Doll Beings

Lillian White – Production Assistance, Goodwill Ambassador
Youth Insights Artists, Contributors of Slide Imagery (Aneka, Angela, Chelsea, Clara, Diana, Irving, Jaylene, John, Laura, Lilly, Mara, Maxine, Minu, Miyani, Onaje, Seth, and Zachary)
Baille Younkman – Costume Assistance
Molly Zimmelman – Manager of the Stage, Exalted Leader of the Way Back to the High Road

In August of 2019, I began archiving the production materials from a recently-completed project, called *12 Shouts to the Ten Forgotten Heavens*, which had been a three-year cycle of twelve healing performance rituals commissioned by the Whitney Museum of American Art in NYC. It began on the Vernal Equinox, March 2016, and recurred on every Solstice and Equinox through December 2018. Each ritual was immersive, site-specific, and durational, and, all together, the cycle included the work of more than 80 collaborators over the course of the twelve performances. The rituals occurred at the exact moments of each respective seasonal turning, which sometimes happened in the middle of the night, or before dawn, or on days when the museum would ordinarily be closed.

○

The rituals we performed—some invented, others gleaned from universal ritual structures—included those of grief and mourning, fertility, purification/cleansing, apology, appeals for consent, appeals for the re-ordering of power, establishing conscious communication with natural elements, sacrifice of perfectionism, visioning/envisioning for the Earth, affirmations of deeper community roles, uncovering the mechanism of truth, reconnecting with ancestral memory, acknowledgement of the presence of magic, acknowledgement of the personhood of the other-than-human, rewriting religious laws to make them more fair, expressing gratitude, displaying beauty, recognizing and accepting responsibility, offering childhood memory to an alternate mythic order, co-exploration of mutual inner landscape, and spiritual rescue operations.

○

Frank Hentschker had cautioned me against just leaving the project behind and moving on to the next and next and next thing. He told me about Friedrich Wilhelm Heinrich Alexander von Humboldt, who took one five-year ship trip to study the natural phenomena of the Americas, and then spent the better part of the rest of his life and career documenting, reflecting upon, and describing his findings. The example came at a crucial moment when I was feeling at a loss for what to do next.

○

Later in the year, I was lucky enough to be granted a residency at the newly-established Centre for Dramaturgy and Curation at the remarkable Siteworks, in the Brunswick neighborhood of Melbourne, Australia. There I began sorting through the digital detritus of the performances, writing reflections on the *Shouts*, their manifestation, and expanding the mythological elements woven throughout the piece. Daniel Owen at Ugly Duckling Presse had invited me to make the pamphlet. I realized that it would be a good way to shelter the creative excess of the project, preserve it in a more lasting medium, and take the first steps toward the life's work that Dr. Hentschker had suggested. Calling it a "religious pamphlet" is a way of doubling down on an expression of belief and faith in the possibilities the *Shouts* were proposing, and in the vision which our imaginations collaborated to put forth.

CDC, Melbourne, August 2019.

Alexander von Humboldt und Aimé Bonpland in der Urwaldhütte by Eduard Ender

As we begin any kind of particular sifting-through, we try to set some Goals beforehand, in order to keep organized. It's not completely necessary, but it keeps authorities happy.

- Video prep: release forms etc.
- Website update—photos, bios etc.
- Catalogue Paula's photos
- Transfer everything from phone & email
- Write reflections (put in Ugly Duckling pamphlet?)
- Set the mythology—tracing the lines of re-telling
- Work with Kate on book layout.

Day 1, July 29th, 2019

A cruel twist at the outset, not all the pics are attaching to the emails from phone to exclusive email address, and many seemed to be lost.

Worst of all the photos documenting the Adonia pots being fired in the backyard at the Aframe. I'm underslept & behaving stupidly. I became seized with a kind of reverse greed around clearing out my phone. Need to show up for this work! But also am a little shocked that the Merc Retro energy is turning against me when what I am doing is what Merc Retro is all about, which is sifting through stuff from the past! Still, perhaps I was being too quick about it and need to keep with a slow plodding energy.

Nevertheless, I did manage to get through the Spring Equinox 2016 and Summer Solstice 2016 *Shouts*.

An interesting quandary that's come up is how much "aftermath" or "blessings"/"gifts" to include. And the spillage into my personal life and health. I suspect these boundaries will become more and more fuzzy as time goes on in the tracking of the project.

Another something I'm encountering is the desire to organize pics from other projects. And I'm shocked at how much I have had going on in the last three years without a break. Surgeries, injuries, getting the house on the market, selling the house, moving house, other projects, elections, travels, visits, sasquatch investigations, fires, relationships, couch surfing/lite homelessness, fundraisers/telethons, and the adventures, social life (resist though I might), and repose of my dog who is with me through it all. Downtimes in between projects are crammed with family obligations which often involve a lot of demanding highway driving and particularized energetic and emotional attention.

Lovely people here in the house @ the CDC/Siteworks doing inspiring, world-changing work. Honored to be here with them. The energy reminds me of New Dramatists. It lends itself to the work and is very supportive and encouraging of one to spread out and breathe into one's work. A real gift.

Day 2, July 30th, 2019

Interested in the discernible pattern of making that can be traced through the photos for each *Shout*.

○

In categorizing I am finding that there is something in between

- Research and
- Production and
- Marketing photos.
- Something that spans all three and so doesn't fit into any of the other ones.
- It's like: Inspiration photos.
- Or: Meaning photos.

Today I emailed up through Winter 2016 to the *12 Shouts* email account. All 2016 photos/vids for *12 Shouts* were emailed from my phone.

Also I arranged and organized the external hard drive so everything is nice and neat and clear, ready to receive incoming.

I downloaded from the *12 Shouts* email account all photos up through Summer 2016.

○

- First thing tomorrow: sort out everything that's in the Downloads folder.
- Then: continue emailing up through Summer 2017.
- Then: download from the *12 Shouts* email account at least the remainder of 2016, if not thru Summer 2017.
- Maybe set up a slide show and begin writing down reflections.

○

One thing that's sticking out continually: how much of my actual life is sagging into the material of the *12 Shouts* project. What is it? Is it desperation? Lack of resources? Lack of seriousness as an artist? Or is it just part of the work and that's what makes the work? It is joyful, though I keep remembering how exhausted I was. The parts of my life that sag into the *Shouts* are the most joyful, even though the parts that aren't are also meaningful. I just can't believe how much else I'm doing besides the work that is my work.

Day 3, July 31st, 2019

Cleaned out the Downloads folder. Yay! This is all I've loaded to the computer, plus downloads of everything from the entire year.

Emailed up to beginning of Summer 2017 but the phone is petering out. I'm going to let it rest today and if it's still giving me a problem tonight/tomorrow I'll resort to 100%

Airdropping, which would be a disappointment (because I won't have a backup other than the drive) but let's see.

Moved everything up to that point into the external drive, and it needs to be sorted.

Leaving a bit early today—there's a lot of noise & commotion here all day and it's making me antsy. Though I was antsy to begin with. Very cranky. Today the Crone has demented to the Hag.

No chance to reflect, just wanting all this loading to be done.

o

Tonight / Tomorrow:

- o Sort all the stuff that's in the external drive.
- o Get (either by email or Airdrop) everything transferred to downloads folder / external drive through Spring 2018.
- ** I think it will be a good idea to do one *Shout* at a time, completely, from here on. Sending, transferring, labeling, sorting. That way it's all clear. I'm starting to get a little muddy (I remember feeling that way at this point in the project as well—Summer 2017 was the halfway point!)

Day 4, August 1st, 2019

Having a claustrophobic feeling with this stuff, like it's bottlenecking or something; it's overwhelming. I felt the same way with the project itself at times—so much of the time, in fact! Any distraction suddenly becomes actually painful. So I took a little mental break this morning and I am moving slower today rather than faster. Also Mercury Rx is giving me such a hard time with this transferring stuff. Now trying to do just a little bit at a time and hoping that will suffice.

The emailing of pictures function is now failing completely, and the Airdrop function doesn't seem too happy either. Just as I was figuring out a new way—Airdropping a few at a time and preparing a new folder so that groups of photos can be dropped in labelled as they come—all of my photos disappeared off of my phone. This puts a very dark feeling in the pit of my gut. I've fiddled around with the iCloud settings (I have avoided iCloud because it makes me so suspicious but it might end up saving the day here) which brought a few photos back from 2006–2015 and it is saying "restoring" with a spinning pinwheel of death and a ". . ."

I have my doubts. Letting it run for now and hoping for the best.

If they're gone, so much will have been lost. But it's SO MUCH. What will/would I *do* with it all? Have been feeling overwhelmed about the whole thing—choked by this bottleneck feeling. Blocked. What is this life that allows for no sorting, sifting, reflection, concluding? I know this is only a week but I'd planned so much more for this time and am just under halfway through the transfers. Because of the way the phone works, there would have been no way to do it quickly.

Ok I think it is indeed coming back. And I think I see part of what the problem is—it's still holding on to deleted photos? I'm looking at "Albums" and the numbers are climbing. This is so stressful, having hope.

There seems to be a message here in all this but what is it? Am I putting my attention in a wrong place? But it does feel important to go through this stuff. Just hanging on, hanging in there, watching them come back, hopefully I'll be able to access them. Jeez Louise! It's a nailbiter!

HARBINGERS & GIFTS

These are signs that show that the change of season is coming. Often it is a sign of the coming season—a snow squall in October, for instance.

Or the spider that appeared in my car right after Summer 2018 that was also a harbinger of Autumn. Harbingers and Gifts often have connections to meanings, research objects, and subject matters within the *Shouts* themselves. Harbingers come before work has begun on the *Shout*, Gifts come immediately afterward and often keep on coming. Finding mushrooms, having experiences with opals, oysters, the coming of looms, deer skulls with egg cocoons embedded, seeds of particular flowers—all are examples of what carries significance from one *Shout* to another. The gifts are what made me realize that the *Shouts* were transforming me and my relationship to my natural home. My huge family, my Ecology Body.

They both contain messages. And those messages are subtle, and I would likely not be able to recognize them as well or as immediately or as consciously before I worked on the *Shouts*.

○

Ok VISITING. Everything starts with a visit.

A visit to Tom's house in Dallas.

A visit to the Watermill Center.

Tom's visit to my house in PA.

A site visit at the Whitney. This was always one of the first things to happen, often coupled with a production meeting and even a budget meeting. These were always incredibly stressful for me, for I was inexperienced and am very sensitive. I perceived the whole thing as an interrogation. I was asked many pointed and detailed questions that I could not possibly have the answer to.

In the instance of a visit, you show up knowing very little. When you show up, you are the Virgin. You've got an open heart and enthusiasm. Chances are good that you're going to get ripped apart in some way. You'll be rejected from the love affair. You'll be scolded for not giving proper notice. You'll be catechized for information you can't possibly yet know.

But if you can get through this stuff—and that is often by performing a mental wellness you do not really experience—the visit can be very meaningful.

The visits people did to me at my house seem to have been the least painful. For me at least. Probably those visiting are the ones being ripped apart though.

How are artists supposed to make it through the making of their work, emotionally? Is it really so corporate?

To this problem, Amanda and especially Greta brought a great deal of humanizing support and understanding. They held that sensitivity in a way I couldn't see then. I see now how they protected me from the harshness of the institution and continually bolstered the vision that wanted to come through. I can never know the risk that meant for them in their jobs and they have my admiration, thanks, and indebtedness forever.

○

The photos are recovered. Even the ones that I thought I'd lost a few days ago of the Adonia pots and Adonia beauty dance. Miracles happen. Looks like the phone holds deleted photos for 30 days after they are deleted.

○

Giving thanks.

RESEARCH

Research comes before the visit too, but the project doesn't really really start until after the visit. The research is wild and it is kind of everything. I follow my nose like a pig who digs up truffles out of the leafs and soil. I can't get enough.

WRITING

Not a lot of photo evidence of this component. But I'm including some of the research and dramaturgy. I know that it happened slowly and with great consideration at first, and well ahead of the event, but without enough information. As the project lived on, the writing happened very quickly and came from a place that was not intellectual. Which was a relief.

PRODUCTION

Production includes rehearsals and planning. In the case of the *12 Shouts*, which were a site-specific set of ritual performances where we could hardly ever, if at all, rehearse at the actual site, a lot of the planning happened in the theoretical imagination. We would have to do it as a group. Before we knew the building very well, and before we had earned the trust and complicity of the Whitney staff. It was maddening. I can still feel the stomach ache these sessions gave me.

Production also included gathering & making props, relics, and sacred ceremonial objects. We would set aside one or two rehearsal days for the making of props (see below also). These days are documented in the photos at Abrons and some at my A-frame house in PA as well.

MORE WRITING

This part was more in a panic sort of mode where I would update the script according to discoveries we'd made in rehearsals.

PROPS

This is where everyone came together and often there were shenanigans because we were just making props together and our minds were free after so much stressful concentration and hypothesizing around unknowns. Props making happened many times in the hallway outside our Abrons office, because the office itself was so hilariously small.

TRANSPORT

This could be a stressful or a joyful time. There are few photographs, but I have many memories of packing and unloading, taking stuff here or there. Picking stuff up or dropping stuff off. Truck and van rentals, but mostly my Subaru Forester, Wayne Frank. Fender benders, getting pulled over by the cops (those often happened with

Suzanne in the car for some reason). There are a couple of very special photos of Molly and Rey in my car. Rey loves Molly and so do I, and she was always so breezy and fun to ride around with, and to do everything with. She made the shows happen every bit as much as I did. And we had a lot of our most meaningful exchanges while transporting stuff around. She wasn't the best at packing. One time I found one of our sacred religious texts (which we made from a leather-bound Bible printed in old Czech that had been a gift from Ariana Truman from some repository of ancient books in Minneapolis, MN) in a thin canvas tote with a bunch of larger river stones on top. I was like, "Molly!!!?" and she was like "What!?" I was so insistent about packing yet could never get organized enough for things to be art-handled in a better way. Even though the Whitney gave us this whole sweet workshop with Jason, one of their best and nicest art handlers, showing us their moves and how-to's. It was one of my failures as a leader, and Molly often bore the brunt of this sad, sloppy, stuck neurosis I would get into. Sometimes I would strategize to get the packing-up done myself so I could let my ground-level poorly prepared but obsessive packing compulsions hold full sway. Then she would come after it was all ready and we would just load up and go. And transport, once we were loaded up, was always fun and the heaviness would be released and there were times when she and Rey would have to share the front seat and they were very cute doing so, and for some reason Molly didn't mind and I know Rey didn't—he loves her.

COSTUMES

The costumes were so important on so many levels because they encouraged/convinced/forced people to let go of any ego attachment around their appearances, general performance presentation, and presentation of self. I'm talking about performers *and* audience. And Whitney staff too. The costumes magically made actorly vanity disappear out the window. And for the audience, it set them at ease in the fancy building. There were details and thoughts to look into in the costumes, and it wasn't threatening because it was all ultimately ridiculous. The costumes set the tone. And so we were able to slip the arguments of the piece under the door where the participants would find and open them. The costumes were the grease-covered package that slipped easily through the drafty crack.

Suzanne and I were always the most successful when she would take the general concepts, themes, and elements at work for one of the *Shouts* and then she could just go to town interpreting that however she saw fit or was already thinking about in the aesthetic inquiry of her own work. The costumes spoke their own language and told their own version of the story, without winking at the audience, because they were so full-on, such a total 100% commitment. It was impossible to argue with them because they were impervious to the application of linear logic, and anyway they were so insane and funny that there really was no reason to want to argue with them. They were a constant reconfiguration.

About halfway through the course of the project I started to get specific costume or character ideas in my mind, and I became more picky and demanding about how the costumes needed to function. Around the same time Suzanne was starting to get very busy with her own work, communication became spotty, and I ended up swooping in, along with the performers themselves, to Save the Deer Women, so to speak. Molly Lieberman and Theodora Lang, Suzanne's daughter, were instrumental in making things happen during times of pinched tightness. In the end, it mostly worked out. The costumes were, in pretty much every instance, the main triumph of the *Shouts*.

TECH

This was where everything broke down, namely myself. This is where the people working on the piece would bifurcate and amplify to complete the work of the piece, because I would reach a point where I could not go any further. I had no more ideas about how to solve the problems I had created in writing and staging a site-specific piece that could not actually be made or rehearsed on-site, and it would become painfully clear that the whole piece was doomed if I were to be left as its leader. And that's where each person would have to pick up a glue gun, or a roll of tape, or a lighting grid, or an audience herding scheme and make it happen. 'Cause I would be done, buddy. And esp. with my interpersonal and communication skills. I would not even be able to form sentences after a while, and people like Bobby would need to say to me, "Sibyl, remember that it ALWAYS WORKS OUT." This is the stuff that now, in hindsight, I am most grateful for, the people who were involved and who *actually made it happen*, and this is also where I doubt myself as an artist.

PERFORMANCE

And in the end, Bobby was right, it always worked out. And it was gorgeous every time, and its only happening once only added to the magic of timing and event and ceremony reverberating into some other plane that we can't yet determine. There was a palpable shift in energy, a transformation, an exchange, and—I hope, because this was the whole point as far as I was concerned—a reciprocation. "Where are we bringing this thing?" or "Where are we sending this thing?" was and is always the most important question. Everything happened in the performance exactly as it needed to. It drained us of anything we might have had left, but it also filled us back up with something else. We would be aglow at the end of it in a way that wasn't just about doing "a show." It was some kind of love that was larger than loving just people, though they were included in it too. We never wanted to hang out with anyone much after—audience or family or anything. I don't know why. We tended to come upstairs and finish the wine in the education room ourselves. Sometimes I would have a feeling like there was a hot air balloon expanding and rising in my solar plexus. The rest of my body would be relaxed.

STRIKE

We got better at this as we went along? I was always a mess at strike; it felt violent. I was so tired, and I would feel torn apart having to face the tearing down, the packing, and the loading, which was the worst. But sometimes it was peaceful and orderly. Strike was always very telling. I should go through and try to remember each one and track how it all developed. The tough ones probably were not even photographed because they were so difficult and painful. It might have just been me that was suffering—though probably the others suffered having to deal with me.

AFTERMATH

These are events that happen. Sometimes it's a party. Sometimes it's the burning of ceremonial objects like scrolls, footnotes, or brooms. Sometimes it's physical injury that hobbles SK or at least causes serious bruising, usually slowing her down where she was unable to slow down previously. But often enough, they are blessings or gifts...

BLESSINGS / GIFTS

These are moments that come up immediately following a *Shout* that are a full expression of everything that was talked about for the upcoming season. Usually it is some kind of pronouncement of Earth, Nature, or Cosmos. Sunlight, plants, animal presence, promulgations of sky or wind.

SHENANIGANS

This is where we blow off steam and fool around. These are sometimes tied to the Afterparties / Aftermath, but often they are before the *Shout* happens, like at Props making day, or, in the instance of the first production meeting for Summer 2018 (the one on the boat), at the production meeting itself. They are always joyful—full of love, and hilarity. Love and hilarity, I'm realizing as I write this, are almost inseparable for me. They bubble up out of some ancient time when life was simpler and more loving. And hilarious.

Day 5, August 2nd, 2019

Visit today from Kiera Brew Kurec. Many insights from her as always, and insights from myself as I am talking with her. She is a most valuable friend and art compadre. Wonderful to have her here when I had been here via Skype with her during her residency.

Her suggestions:

- Annotations of each image. Lots more work of course, but could be recorded and then transcribed later. (So that if for some reason I am separated from them, they could clarify how one can mediate them.)
- Reflections from all participants.
- Get everything organized.
- Take everyone in groups of seven for three days (14 ppl) each to Mt. Tremper.

- Show them all the images.
- Everybody writes.
- One hour a day tending to it, and nurturing it.
- One day a month tending to it, and nurturing it.
- Look into archiving funding—institutions, foundations.
- Talk to Clay Hapaz
- Talk to archiving guy (David?) at the Whitney
- Great project for Mercury Rx.

○

I've gotten through sending (either by email or by Airdrop when email can't do it any longer) pics from up to Autumn 2018. Almost there! Tomorrow I can finish in the first part of the day.

I think then I want to take a closer look at this Virgin book. And use that as a way to frame the process of each *Shout*. I really think there's something there.

○

Tomorrow:

- Clear & sort Downloads folder contents.
- Download emailed pics from today.
- Email Fall 2018 & Winter 2018.
- Sort downloaded pics.
- Download emailed pics.
- Sort Downloads folder.
- Read Virgin book.
- Reflect. Record?

Day 6, August 3rd, 2019

Ok, almost done, starting to mix in some reflections here.

○

Summer 2018 was so great because Amanda Davis could relax, and we all could kind of relax, because it was on a boat! And because, by then, her conversion from Whitney staffer/artwork protector to fully-indoctrinated Daughter of Eve was complete.

Looking at the photos of Summer Solstice 2018 the BRIDGES seem very significant.

- Upper Deck Flag Wavers
- Medicine Wheelers
- Milkweed Wind Wishers

○

Just got everything off of my phone.

Overwhelmed by a feeling of sadness. Vivid picture of my Aunt Lauris's account of my Aunt Phyllis's death. The gentle restfulness of it, the slipping away, after everyone who piled in to visit her in her final day had gone.

○

End of day, all is sent, all is downloaded.

Only sorting and putting on hard drive, and more sorting there, remains.

○

Having so many crises of confidence as I go through these.

But I realize that continuing, and the practice itself, is the only thing that can redeem.

Not settling for the situation that is thrown together will be the key to moving forward. There is always plenty to work on in the humane way. In order for love to remain intact, there needs to be ample space. It will be a challenge to break the habitual view that the only way the work can happen is by throwing together.

Day 7, August 4th, 2019

Yesterday I showed Mark the "Invisible Horizon" and it was a meaningful moment. It came in an instant when I was feeling like "What am I doing!!??" and reconnected me with where I am. Thank you, Mark.

○

Shenanigans figure in indirectly. They are expressions of energy and energies of expression that are not directly consequential to or from the actual performance itself. They are extras, excesses. Examples of exuberance.

○

SK tech rehearsal gaze, remembering when I was laying back there during Winter 2017 tech after I fell and totally f'd up my shin. I think I was in shock. Elke found me back there. She said the color had drained out of my face completely. The shin still feels weird a year and a half later. Sometimes it is numb and probably still has a scar. There is definitely a dent there. It was like an aftermath injury that occurred early, during tech. It taught me to sit in one place and let everything orbit around me, which—there was a lot going on in that one. The eight hour one with the four set changes. By Spring 2018, there was a lot going on all over again. In my personal life. I think I was probably turning that over as well.

All photos and vids are now transferred to the external hard drive. They need only to be organized.

○

Can we make a positive gene expression through this project?

What is the antidote experience to trauma?

○

"I mustn't be the only one."—Kiera Brew Kurec.

○

When I look through and listen to everything, the things that excite me the most about this project are the things I didn't even do. The sound pieces that Tei made, the costumes that Suzanne made, the musical compositions, the choreography, the performances of the priestesses are all examples. Maybe I worked with them on these things that they made, but they made them. When I go back and re-experience these things, I fill up with so much love I feel like I could explode.

○

I don't know whether it's ok to include all the sound stuff and compositions on the hard drive because of copyright stuff... Lemme check around.

○

Summer was the time of including video in the *Shouts* performances. I think they were always such expansive performances that we needed video to get everything across. We tried to do it for Fall 2018 but it got nixed by Greta because it was too much and there weren't enough resources. I learned at a fundraising event one time that this is known in the curating world as a "talk down"— when you have to talk an artist out of an idea of something they want to do because it is **too much** in some way. It is worth noting that this is the only time during the entire process that Greta Hartenstein tried to talk me out of any of my ideas. No matter how outlandish they were, Greta and the others—especially as the cycle rolled on—found ways of bringing the images that came to me into being, for the sake of the spirit of the piece/s. Even if it meant ferreting out a subversive way around the institutional practices, policies, and procedures that might have blocked us otherwise. Greta was advocate, protector, and supreme supporter of what wanted to come through the artist into the piece, into the museum. She never flinched from being co-agent in the criticality of the institution that we occasioned to voice through our work. I should also like to note here that the Fall 2019 *Shout* ended up being, and remains, my favorite one, even without the stinkin' Southfork video.

○

With regard to ritual practice itself. We didn't know what we were doing. We had ideas, but were afraid to follow through with them. We would feel something start to happen—right away when we would do the clapping for "Never follow a hippie to a second location," for example. We would always back off, because we didn't have a framework in case we actually broke through. I didn't want to see Sarah Willis suddenly crawling up the wall of the Whitney lobby with her parents standing right there watching (this was the worst case scenario that always haunted me). We wouldn't know what to do! Tom was there that first Spring *Shout* and he claimed that he had it handled but I didn't want to test it. Same with the Security Camera Ghost video of Winter 2016, the mantras of Spring 2017. It was a gesture, but not a full conjuring. With time we built that framework, and I learned more and was able to secure more guidance. Stuff started to HAPPEN. We felt it, and saw it again and again. It was a conversation between the participants of the ritual, and things that would happen afterward in 'Nature'—which included our own feelings and also events or occurrences that one could now recognize as not-random. Our actions and our thoughts have power beyond what Western industrialized thought acknowledges. It became clear that human feelings are part of Nature and that they were part of our interaction with phenomena of Nature. We interacted and influenced those phenomena through our ritual actions and thought forms, which were their own language. We began to recognize the patterns of communication in coincidental events and occurrences that transpired around the rituals, which required only our full presence and active attention to be understood. In this way, there were no limits to the extent to which everything lives and speaks. We began to see this during the course of our work on this project. We are only limited by the quality of our attention.

August 6th, 2019

THE INVISIBLE HORIZON. A RELIGIOUS PAMPHLET.

○

This is my new idea that was handed to me through talking with Mark, and asking for help from my ancestors in knowing what the hell to do.

○

We stand at the bank of a great and mighty river, staring out into a blank expanse before us. We know, in our hearts and in our deep memory, that there is a vista here, of mountains and rocks and trees on the other side, on the opposite bank. We know that time is running out. We know we have to do something, and that it has to be an action taken now. But our thoughts are clouded by the finest mist of strong emotions. We cannot see the way forward. We stand at the West, the place of our soul's true purpose, gazing into the blank distance toward a new beginning to the East. We stand, looking. We are not holding our breath but we might as well. Truly these conditions are the very best for setting intentions. The relative solidity and stillness of the atmosphere will hold them fast. And when things start moving again, when the winds, breezes of change begin once again to blow, the potency that has built up from those intentions during this time of stillness, blindness, and stagnation will move and spread quickly through space and across lands. So. Now. What do we mean to do? What is it. That we mean to do.

○

And we have to get this really clear before we can move forward.

○

We mean to change the world, of course. We mean to change the course of the world. We intend to reattach the outer world to the inner one, the surface world to the world of deepness, our present experience to the deepest memories and to the farthest flung futures. We mean to embody the noblest _____ of everyone who came before, and in the name of everyone who comes after. To begin enacting a more meaningful way of being alive. We mean to wake to our finest destiny. To remember, and to help others remember, all of the connections that allow us to be here. To remember that there is no separation of mind and body, of self and surroundings.

○

We intend to change the story, to rewrite the old stories, to rewrite the laws. We mean to quell our anger with a sound application of justice. We mean to re-include the stuff that was edited out, the stuff that provides balance. We mean to reconnect with our deeper roles in the community. We mean to reestablish the community. We resolve to encounter, and to embrace, the Other, who resides within ourselves.

○

We use the wisdom of our hearts and the vision of our deepest memory to navigate the way forward. And we trust that all will become clear. In a nick of time.

○

What you can't see is the outcome, the impact. We might not be able to see it in our lifetime. So that makes it hard sometimes. We have got to keep envisioning it for ourselves.

○

This is the deeper side, the one that didn't get enough immediate attention because of the logistics that were needed to make everything happen and to make all the love come out. In order to ensure that we were moving toward the light, we had to ensure that we were working together. Which was not always easy to achieve or maintain. The bonds that form in that effort—of overcoming the difficulties of working together—are very strong. I believe that willingness is what will ultimately save us from destruction, if anything does or can. The forces of evil cannot overcome those difficulties because they can ultimately only serve themselves. Any alliances must be temporary. For this reason, it is worth the trouble. The decision to overcome those difficulties is the decision to love.

○

The clock is ticking, but it is ticking softly, in a quiet room made of very old wood. It is a winter's day and there is a stained glass window that looks out onto an old school yard. Heat comes from three quartz crystal cylinders in the old fireplace. Here the clock ticks. It ticks quietly, pleasantly. You hear the passing of a train in the distance. And the clock is ticking. You are safe. And the clock is ticking.

○

And whatever we do in the end, it will be and will have been better than nothing.

POST-RESIDENCY RETROFLECTIONS.

I knew a girl in school who was very special, a little stand-offish, sometimes even off-putting, because she came from Atlantis, the lost city. If she ever looked at you, it was easy to accept—for in the gaze of her eyes was a tenderness and sympathy that often seemed barely possible. I knew that she had continued her work in our own society, trying to help, healing what wounds she could with the power of understanding. There was also great wisdom and the power of judgement. Again, it wasn't easy. The sunken city. Her name was Omie. I contacted her. She assembled the charts of the constellations and planets and interpreted their signals in the cosmological moments. They came through in combinations of concepts and qualities that formed images. It was delicate work, describing the movements of the firmament in images, translated to poetic language and recognizable to humans—like filigree. I worked with those images, weaving them into the narrative or making them happen literally, using rudimentary materials like plastic, hot glue, processed cheese products, pantyhose, foam rubber, faux fur, animal bones, pleather, cellulose.

○

From her underwater home, her distant cousins followed. Merche, with the technologies to communicate with whales, clickety shrimp, dolphins, and with Neptune and all the other water goddesses. And Darlene, with special knowledge about the secrets of plants, about the way their seeds hold the embryos of the plants which could just as well be animal, or human. And of what the plants have to offer us in the future and on a very deep level. And her two boyfriends and helpers, Tei and Sean, both of whom have special knowledge and teachings to share with humanity moving forward. There is a film of them all dancing in the Atlantean way on the lower sternward deck of the Harbor Lights, the damp gray city passing by in the background.

○

We call in the grace, strength, and beauty of the female cardinal. The one whose tail feathers are the color of the lightning coming over the hills above the Hudson River farther North into the dramatic mountains where I now live when I am home. The compact, the adorable. The generous and loving. The warmth. The willingness to stay.

○

We call in the grace, majesty, and fierceness of the great blue heron. The spread of huge wings of the lightest weight and exquisite variation of subtle color in its feathers, the glowing yellow eye with a deepset soul in its pupil, the expressive angle of beak, the patience, the seizing of opportunity in a flash of knowing. The elegant shoulders, and so the elegant relationship to the elders. The hollow bones to allow one to commune with highest thoughts. The reminder to always make sure you've got consent before you take the wings.

○

We call in the help and wisdom of Great Grandmother Groundhog, with the beautiful eyes, who we see standing in the overgrown backyard, looking around. Great Grandmother Groundhog, you are wise and know to never run into the road. You are the matriarch of so many groundhogs in this tiny city where I now live in the North, and you are intelligent, alert, and yet unperturbed. Bring us underground with you, so that we may experience the consciousness that is underneath. Lead us to the underworld, and keep us safe. We set up the boundaries and we prepare to do the hard work. We tuck our shirts into our underwear, and roll up our sleeves, and prepare to work hard toward an accomplishment that is big and important. *Zagushtun*, as is said in Bulgaria.

○

On the East side of the River, I spent one Winter of firsthand learning about Mary and the Christ. The Christ was also a Mayan King who was not so much crucified as became one with a tree, sort of like Daphne but not as an escape from anything, and then burned and burned with a passionate longing for Justice, revealing a pterodactyl skeleton that rose from the flames. They were harsh and glorious lessons, which were completed in Spring 2018, through Oya, the great buffalo vulva goddess, who came in the form of a literal and emotional tornado and reordered the power structures. We tributed Mary as goddess of changing forces, a moon with sharp teeth, a birth-sex-death deity and ultimate catch in the Universe, of patience that could not be challenged. We gifted her by letting go. By disappearing like a palomino trout does in the waters of well-boundaried and yet boundless creativity.

○

We are the Hero and we are also the Virgin. Our journey is outward and inward at the same time. We give and we receive. We move into the future and into the very distant past.

○

We called on many women who were living and thriving in caves. We asked them to come forward and make vessels and remake the world. Mary Magdalene, The Virgin Mary, the Lady Sasquatch, and others.

○

Red Moon Lilith was living in the desert, working with vibrations. We called her in to help us retell the whole story. She was bitter at having been left out of Paradise. And aren't we all. And we're not sure we gave her a real fair shake at justice or at redefining herself. Though she certainly did justice to history, rewriting the religious laws together with Eve, balancing them and making them more fair. As Omie predicted. She swooped in at the last possible and repeating moments of suicide and saved all the Misses Julies, her representatives who dare to enjoy sexuality as separate from procreation.

○

And there were women we called in who were living in other wildernesses: Shamhat, who had saved the wild man Enkidu from domestication, sickness, and death, and who together with Enkidu had successfully gone back in human narrative and wilded Gilgamesh the King, and had turned him to choose Love instead of reject it, and to give the seed of his body to the goddess of Love rather than withhold it from her, and to turn away from the ridiculous idea of immortality and re-submit to the cycles of the Moon. In these choices, Gilgamesh freed his predecessor Adam, the first man, from being such a dick to Lilith and really also to Eve, and God, and the Garden, and also freed his successor, Harry Whitney, from all the greed and priggishness and prissiness of a man with too much attention to money and too little sense of his deeper role in the community. These were the fruiting bodies of the mycelium of Man. And brave Bobby, hero embodying all these heroes, submitting again and again, and publicly, to the ancient will of the Moon Cycles, and forcing and encouraging and convincing, and overwhelming, and embracing the other males to do the same, and especially the other white males, and to deepen their hearts and step forward, display their beauty as physical and moral specimens. And sharing in his role of the Adonis, our beautiful teacher, with Brandon, who rose at Springtime from the assembled bones of everything beautiful that was lost that year before its time, and mourned in the Summer, and resurrected again in the Spring.

○

We called in two young women from Outer Space who both had a connection to Atlantis. Maria and Leonie. They reconstructed the Healing Temple of the Violet Flame. They knew about the Healing Temple because they had communicated with it from the UFO which hovered over its exact location on the ocean floor. The waves were turbulent of course. But deep down, the Violet Flame of the Healing Temple of Atlantis can never be extinguished. We know it deep down, because it burns deep down.

○

There are four other women, who are part of the outer space part of this equation, or are connected to that part of the equation, and those women are able to distinguish between themes, concepts, topics, and images.

○

The spill-proof cup may have gone against its making and spilled out all over the contents of the bag, but that worst possible moment was also the best possible moment. For all present.

○

We hope, we hope we hope. We never stop trying. We remember to look to the spiritual when we are impoverished, and we give self-love, which brings us through.

○

Leonie and Maria were a different, but related group of Outer Space People, to those extra-terrestrial visitors who brought us not only the boletes, but the rhizomatic potatoes who were made into our beloved Potato Doll Beings, who are still working to change everything and are succeeding. May we ever seek their blessings and be sure to take the Potato Doll Beings out at least once or twice a year, in the cooler weather of Autumn Equinox and the colder weather of Winter Solstice, to be danced and honored and festooned and fed and fêted.

○

The opals. The dragonflies. The oyster shells. Those clearing, iridescent energies that turn to snow in the doorways, and rise through the floors of the museum along with the smoke from the ceremonial protest sage burning, from the banners and the visions of forgotten heavens, the ones beside the one next door and the one containing God. Our visions of them. Our conceptions received in our imaginations. The ones that clear the tears from the tear gas, and clear the clouded vision of those in charge who have the power to change the structures but have refused to see the need, and wipe the sacred tears of those whose ancestors were destroyed on their own land, and whose ancestors were brought here against their will, and of those who come to this land seeking a better life and with so much to give.

○

And the sacrificial ox of Autumn, adorned with the flowers of late summer, and adored by all, set into a life of hard labor and offered up in muscular beauty for the sake of a great awakening. Presented in innocence in the open field.

○

The great and mighty family clan who buys the house back from the bank, who keeps secret wealth because of the skill of an ancestor, and who gathers together in ceremony to burn the purchased work of imposters.

A NOTE ON THE TEAR GAS.

To me the crisis was & is not just a political but a spiritual one. It is about the shortage of love that has been exacerbated by globalization. When the news broke about Warren Kanders, my first impulse was to pull the final, twelfth *Shout*. Because that gassing of men, women, and children at the border, and in Ferguson, and at Standing Rock (and, as I write this, in so many cities across the U.S. in atrocious reaction to the uprisings against racism and police brutality), and the Whitney's connection to it went against *everything* the *Shouts* were about! I was like, "How could we possibly do it now?" I don't know whether any of Kanders' money directly funded my project. I don't think it did—he was more interested in backing the big ones, like the Warhol exhibit next door, for example. But that whole staircase out of the main lobby, where we had reenacted a baroque rendering of The Triumph of the Dominican Order, is the "Allison and Warren Kanders Staircase." We were seized with horror. The artist MPA's "Bloodline" in the Spring of 2017 had been more accurate than anyone could have suspected at the time. There was blood gushing down that staircase where we had worked. We were covered in it—hands and all...

○

Omie, our astrologer, from Atlantis you may remember, had already cast the chart for the Winter Solstice 2018 a long time beforehand, so that we could work with the imagery in the making of the ceremonies for the performance. In going back to that chart we found that one of the transits indicated a revelation of the puppet strings of power—for everyone: a sudden reveal of the ways in which we are connected to world events that we might rather not be. A revelation of our true responsibility and connectedness for well or ill.

The most immediate crisis at that moment was the situation at the border with Mexico. U.S. Border patrol had used tear gas on a group of asylum-seekers at the San Ysidro port of entry between Tijuana and San Diego at the end of November 2018. The group included women and children, whose legitimate paperwork for asylum had been stalled in a purposeful quagmire by the Trump administration. Mostly from Honduras and other troubled Central American countries, they were fleeing violence, poverty, and political persecution. This crisis is ongoing, has since worsened in the separation of children from their families and their imprisonment in reprehensible conditions, and will take generations to heal.

It seemed impossible to 'put on a show' in the midst of this kind of revelation. I did feel, after many conversations with people inside and outside the museum, that we somehow had to finish our project. It seemed to me that there was a reason why this was happening now—and not, say, in the middle or at the beginning of the three-year cycle of our project. It was unfolding at the very end of it, at its culmination. It occurred to me that there was a responsibility placed upon us, to make an offering that simultaneously brought attention to those puppet strings and provided healing, in a ritual context, toward what had taken place. I didn't know how to go forward. I had to feel my way.

"The Invisible Horizon" comes from a photograph that I took at the bank of the Hudson River where I live in Newburgh that usually affords a grand view of the river bank opposite. But the day I was there, right after this whole ugly thing broke and I was trying to figure out what to do, you couldn't see anything because of a fog that was there. And at the same time, within myself, I could not see a way forward.

○

I did some envisioning with my mentor, Donna, and she saw another side of events that would take place four days later at the first protest by Decolonize This Place. I saw the concrete side: the sage burning which was so heavy with smoke that the fire department was called in (I didn't see the fire department part, just the burning of sage in the lobby—a way of clearing bad or stuck energy. I remember thinking, "But we're not allowed to burn anything inside the museum!" Ha ha. Little did I know.). Donna saw two strands of bright iridescent light spiraling up from a place on the floor of the lobby. They came from a place set on a compass of the four cardinal directions, which was surrounded by papers on which people who had come to the *Shouts* had written their visions for the story of the forgotten heavens. She described the strands as dancing and they traveled up the elevator shafts and the staircase into the offices of the floors above. The protest took place four days later, and it turned out that the place in the lobby where the protesters were burning the sage was the same place from which the strands of light that Donna saw had originated. In place of the papers from our audience members were the banners of the protesters. We could hardly believe it. And when I told Greta about this, she told me that indeed, they could smell the sage burning all the way up in their seventh floor offices and above. I also made sure to tell the stunning alignment to the museum's director, whose jaw hit the floor—"That's the same thing that happened with the protesters burning the sage in the lobby!" I also made sure to tell the lead activist from Decolonize This Place. "On some level," I told him, "what you are doing is already working."

Another part of what Donna saw was that there was a fire burning at the center of a large circle of people, and that no two sets of eyes would see the situation from the same angle, in the same way.

○

These "coincidences" (I put the word in quotes because I don't believe they are coincidences at all) confirmed for me that it would be better to do something than nothing, and I resolved to do the *Shout*, with an extra healing ceremony for the sake of what had happened, to occur at the moment of Solstice when we would normally do a bell-ringing ceremony. And on the condition that our performers and participants would be free to speak out against the funding of state violence and the art-washing of profits made from state violence and the Whitney's role in the situation. They agreed, and we constructed an Eye-Washing ceremony to which we invited the Board and all the Whitney Staff. We also obtained stickers, t-shirts, and posters from Decolonize This Place to show solidarity with their efforts during our three-day Retroflective (I borrowed this term from the Mary Corse exhibit on the eighth floor, which had to do with qualities of reflective light).

○

I can't find the written version of what I said at the eye-washing ceremony, but it was something about the land. Asking people how they came to be on this land. Whether it was the rightful land of their people; or whether their predecessors came here as colonizers; or whether their ancestors had been kidnapped from their own land and brought here against their will, as human machines to be bought and sold on which the current economy had been built; or perhaps whether they had come here seeking asylum from another place where there was violence, poverty, or persecution. And what clouded their vision? What was it that blinded each person and kept them from seeing the whole of the truth? Was it tears of grief? Was it desire to maintain comfort, or material wealth, or the status quo that caused their blindness? Was it the tear gas that had been sprayed in the faces of their relations in Ferguson, Standing Rock, or San Ysidro? The day Daniel Owen emailed me about this pamphlet, I had just written this remembrance:

○

I said something... and then we gently washed people's eyes. Brandon Oakes asked permission from Theresa Bear Fox of the Akwesasne Women Singers to sing their women's song in praise of water, and so he accompanied us, with rattles to drive out anything unwelcome or troublesome. We carried prepared fabrics of special significance to the *Shouts* for the task. One had images of the Deer Women (commonly known as 'does') from Autumn Equinox 2017 on the Highline. We had unfurled a length of the fabric at the end of that performance and invited the audience to perform a ritual to free the Deer Women from blood pool hell. The audience members were asked to pour purified water over the images of the Deer Women on the fabric until all the water in the pot was gone. At the Autumn Equinox 2018, that same fabric was rendered into a round target, and Donna shot arrows that had magenta, stuffed, satin stars at their tips at it, symbolizing the becoming of the Deer Women into Ancestors. The star arrows had been based on magic wands that both Omie and I had had as little girls. The same magenta satin from which the stars that Donna had used on the tips of her arrows to shoot at a target made of that Deer Woman fabric at the Autumn Equinox of 2018 were made. We used both scraps from the magenta satin, and the cut-up Deer Women fabric to make the cloths with which we washed people's eyes. We needed some of that magic now. We needed transformation. The fabric was cut into squares, ironed, and folded. I gathered water from a spring near my place in Newburgh, NY, and purified it with tuning forks, using the Solfeggio sound frequencies that we had used in several other *Shouts*, and a group of us donned the Doric chitons from our first Adonia ritual during the Summer Solstice 2016. What felt so heavy at the outset seemed to lift and lighten by the end of our task. After the ceremony we offered the remaining water to the Hudson River across the West Side Highway, which was akin to the water purification rituals we had done in the past.

o

A bunch of us wore the DTP stickers throughout the activities of the three days, plus some "SafariLand" t-shirts that Alexis had obtained. Several performers made statements as part of their Docentry tours, and there were posters available to visitors as they entered the exhibit. We took up a collection for the RAICES organization, which didn't yield very much, disappointingly. I had hoped to put the proceeds of the screening of Masha's video portraits on the final night toward RAICES also, but the museum director decided to just make the event free instead. He was being very careful, I guess.

○

Anyway, I breathed a huge sigh of relief when Warren Kanders finally stepped down from the Whitney Board last July, seven months after our ritual. As I make edits for the text of this pamphlet, the Black Lives Matter protest movement has ignited across the U.S. and Europe, demanding an end not only to police violence, but indeed to the system of policing itself. During this extraordinary time, Warren Kanders, while still siding with law enforcement, announced that his company will no longer manufacture tear gas.

August 31st, 2019

The *12 Shouts* project, as a whole, represents a submission to a ritual cycle—an alignment with the breathing process of the Earth, as Rudolf Steiner would have it. This pamphlet is an experiential record of the flotsam and jetsam that washed up on the shore from the making of that project.

POSTSCRIPT April 16th, 2019.

The wriggling white larvae would stay on/with the land long enough to begin to see that it was alive. They would learn from those who had been there all along, to begin to recognize the Earth as their Life-giver. And to see that it was personal. Each one, one at a time, came to this realization. They began to feel her in their hearts again. They stopped being afraid. They saw how meaningless were the objects. They looked around them and saw how they had destroyed the lives and traditions—both sacred and mundane—of other groups of human people in their greed. It was not easy, for they saw what they had done.

They asked for help as they began to wake up. They woke up crying. They asked for help from their ancestors—the ones from before they had wriggled away from the Earth and become so monstrous. They asked for help from their ancestors from way back in the time before they knew fear, before they fell away from the Earth. The ancestors were glad to be asked, and helped them. They held them while the larvae people cried in shame and anguish. What they approached was not new to them. It was a connection that was lost. They began to regain. To remember. To heal. To clean up the mess. It was just in time. The Earth could still heal and they could still be saved. It was just in time. The Earth could still heal and be saved. They began to feel the Earth again, to see their true relationship with this old, old being, and not to fear the Earth because they thought it was only their Mother.

The ones who did not wake up fell away. They had no power anymore, nobody else cared about their objects. The larvae people stepped back and cared for all the other people—human and otherwise—that they had harmed. They formed cocoons around themselves and their closest loved ones, and in so doing joined the Earth that is so beloved and cared for in the Universe, and all those connected to it, and those they had forcefully torn away from it were also reconnected. They rejoined. The relationship, the balance, the love supply was replenished and restored. This is not like a rejoicing-all-the-time, it isn't a drunken party, it is a sober movement.

Invisible Horizon: A Religious Pamphlet
© Sibyl Kempson, 2020

2020 Pamphlet Series
ISBN 978-1-946433-57-2
First Edition, First Printing
Edition of 1,000

Ugly Duckling Presse
The Old American Can Factory
232 Third Street, #E-303
Brooklyn, NY 11215
uglyducklingpresse.org

Distributed in the USA by SPD/Small Press Distribution
Distributed in the UK by Inpress Books

Series design by chuck kuan and Sarah Lawson
Typeset by Ainee Jeong
Type is New Century Schoolbook
Cover paper and flyleaf from French Paper Co.
Printed offset and bound at McNaughton & Gunn
Flyleaf printed letterpress at Ugly Duckling Presse

This publication is made possible, in part, by support from the New York State Council on the Arts, a state agency. This project is supported by the Robert Rauschenberg Foundation.

This pamphlet is part of UDP's 2020 Pamphlet Series: twenty commissioned essays on poetics, translation, performance, collective work, pedagogy, and small press publishing. The authors are listed below; their pamphlets are available for individual purchase and as a subscription (uglyducklingpresse.org/subscribe). Each offers a different approach to the pamphlet as a form of working in the present, an engagement at once sustained and ephemeral.

Mirene Arsanios
~~Omar Berrada~~*
Sergio Chejfec
Don Mee Choi
Kunci Study Forum & Collective
Iris Cushing
Simon Cutts
Nicole Cecilia Delgado
Adjua Gargi Nzinga Greaves
Dimitra Ioannou

Sibyl Kempson
Claudia La Rocco
Aditi Machado
Chantal Maillard
Tinashe Mushakavanhu
Sawako Nakayasu
Tammy Nguyen
Aleksandr Skidan
Steven Zultanski
Magdalena Zurawski

*Nadine George-Graves & Okwui Okpokwasili

To win a subscription, write to office@uglyducklingpresse.org with your solution to the following puzzle: Using only 6 straight lines, divide the circle on the back cover so that each number is in its own section, without any overlap between numbers.